COLORING BOOKS
FOR GIRLS
ANIMAL DESIGNS

ART THERAPY COLORING

Preview of Coloring Pages

Did You Enjoy Our Coloring Book?

We Want To Hear About It!

Help spread the word about our adult coloring books! We give 10% of all proceeds from Art Therapy products to benefit pancreatic cancer patients and their families.

The best way to spread the word is through reviews. We know how busy you are, especially with all of that coloring, but we would appreciate it!

Visit our website at **www.arttherapycoloring.com**

Visit our website at www.arttherapycoloring.com

Get a Free Printable Coloring Ebook!

We've created an exclusive offer for our customers to receive a free Adult Coloring Ebook.

Visit **www.arttherapycoloring.com/freebie** to claim your free coloring book with over 30 new designs that you can instantly print and color!

Over 100 Art Therapy Coloring Books

See our collection of over 100 Art Therapy Coloring Books for Adults, Men, Seniors, Teens, Kids, Boys, and Girls on the following pages.

Coloring Books For Girls

Coloring Books For Boys

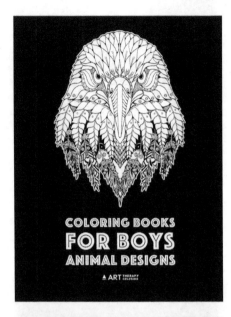

COLORING BOOKS
FOR BOYS
ANIMAL DESIGNS
ART THERAPY COLORING

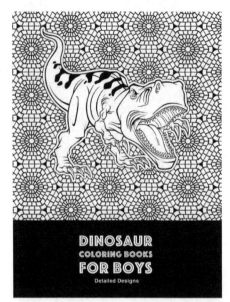

DINOSAUR
COLORING BOOKS
FOR BOYS
Detailed Designs

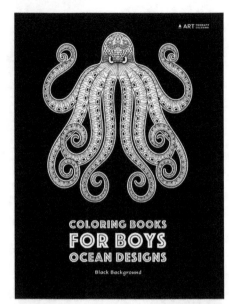

COLORING BOOKS
FOR BOYS
OCEAN DESIGNS
Black Background

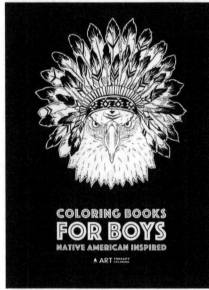

COLORING BOOKS
FOR BOYS
NATIVE AMERICAN INSPIRED
ART THERAPY COLORING

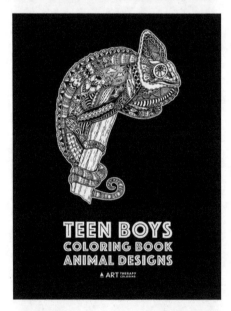

TEEN BOYS
COLORING BOOK
ANIMAL DESIGNS
ART THERAPY COLORING

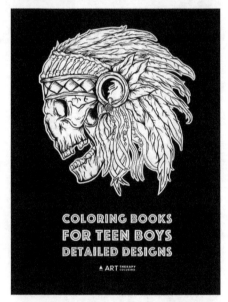

COLORING BOOKS
FOR TEEN BOYS
DETAILED DESIGNS
ART THERAPY COLORING

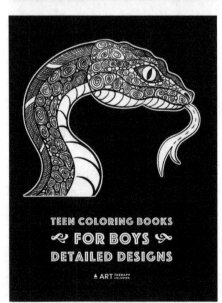

TEEN COLORING BOOKS
FOR BOYS
DETAILED DESIGNS
ART THERAPY COLORING

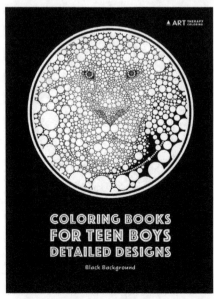

COLORING BOOKS
FOR TEEN BOYS
DETAILED DESIGNS
Black Background

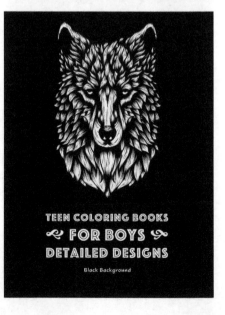

TEEN COLORING BOOKS
FOR BOYS
DETAILED DESIGNS
Black Background

Coloring Books For Kids

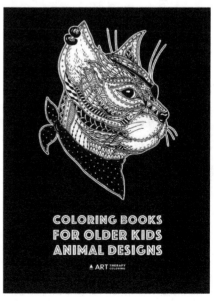

Coloring Books For Teens

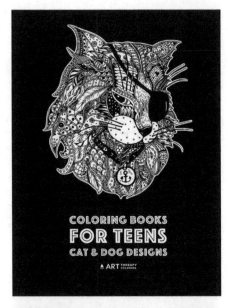

COLORING BOOKS
FOR TEENS
CAT & DOG DESIGNS
ART THERAPY COLORING

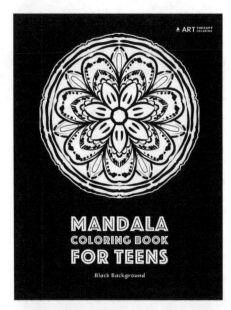

MANDALA
COLORING BOOK
FOR TEENS
Black Background

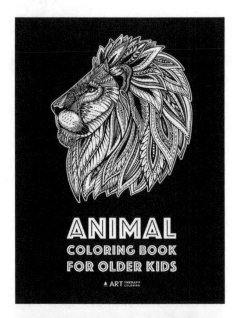

ANIMAL
COLORING BOOK
FOR OLDER KIDS
ART THERAPY COLORING

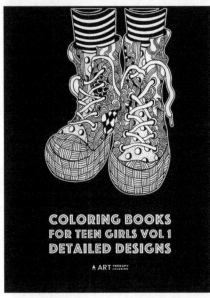

COLORING BOOKS
FOR TEEN GIRLS VOL 1
DETAILED DESIGNS
ART THERAPY COLORING

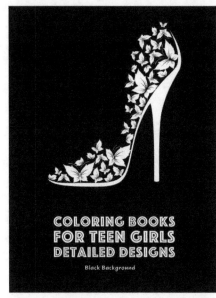

COLORING BOOKS
FOR TEEN GIRLS
DETAILED DESIGNS
Black Background

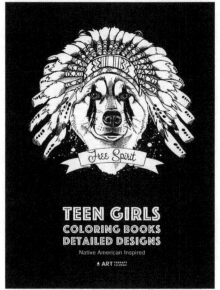

TEEN GIRLS
COLORING BOOKS
DETAILED DESIGNS
Native American Inspired
ART THERAPY COLORING

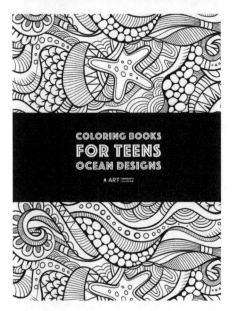

COLORING BOOKS
FOR TEENS
OCEAN DESIGNS
ART THERAPY COLORING

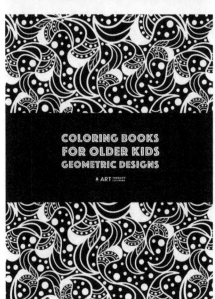

COLORING BOOKS
FOR OLDER KIDS
GEOMETRIC DESIGNS
ART THERAPY COLORING

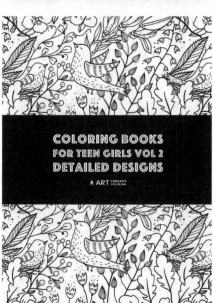

COLORING BOOKS
FOR TEEN GIRLS VOL 2
DETAILED DESIGNS
ART THERAPY COLORING

Coloring Books For Teens

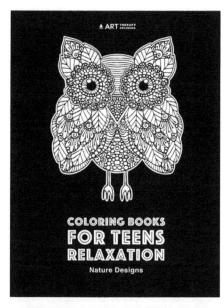

COLORING BOOKS
FOR TEENS
RELAXATION
Nature Designs

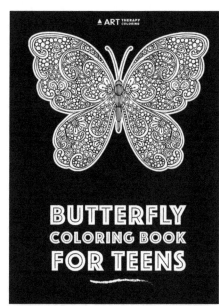

BUTTERFLY
COLORING BOOK
FOR TEENS

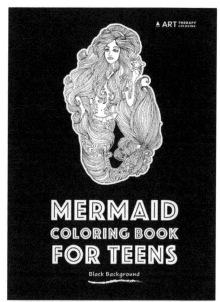

MERMAID
COLORING BOOK
FOR TEENS
Black Background

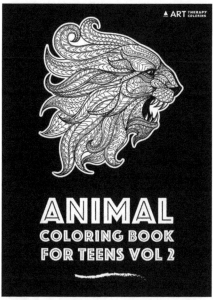

ANIMAL
COLORING BOOK
FOR TEENS VOL 2

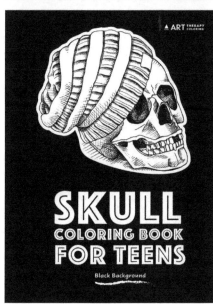

SKULL
COLORING BOOK
FOR TEENS
Black Background

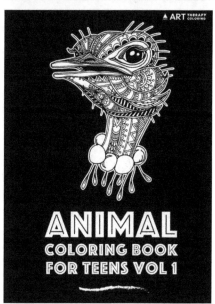

ANIMAL
COLORING BOOK
FOR TEENS VOL 1

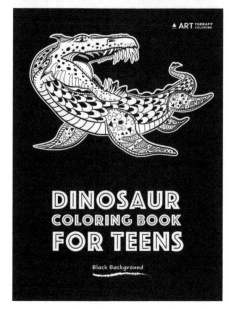

DINOSAUR
COLORING BOOK
FOR TEENS
Black Background

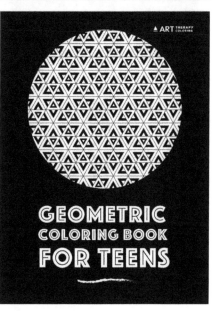

GEOMETRIC
COLORING BOOK
FOR TEENS

MOTORCYCLE
COLORING BOOK
FOR TEENS
Black Background

Coloring Books For Teens

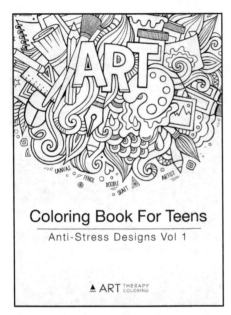

Coloring Book For Teens
Anti-Stress Designs Vol 1

ART THERAPY COLORING

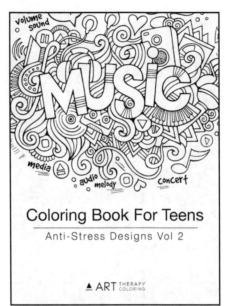

Coloring Book For Teens
Anti-Stress Designs Vol 2

ART THERAPY COLORING

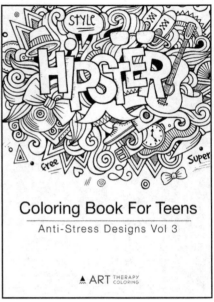

Coloring Book For Teens
Anti-Stress Designs Vol 3

ART THERAPY COLORING

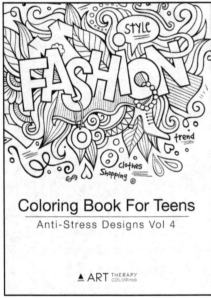

Coloring Book For Teens
Anti-Stress Designs Vol 4

ART THERAPY COLORING

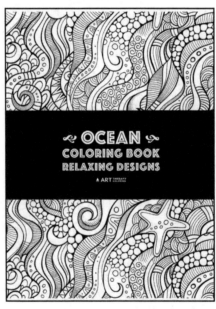

OCEAN COLORING BOOK RELAXING DESIGNS

ART THERAPY COLORING

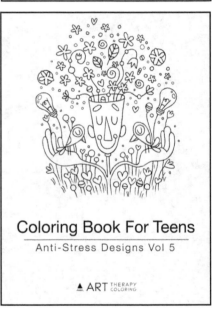

Coloring Book For Teens
Anti-Stress Designs Vol 5

ART THERAPY COLORING

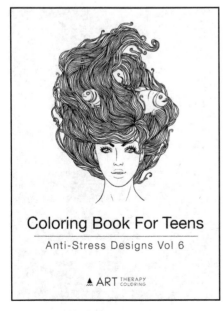

Coloring Book For Teens
Anti-Stress Designs Vol 6

ART THERAPY COLORING

Coloring Book For Teens
Anti-Stress Designs Vol 7

ART THERAPY COLORING

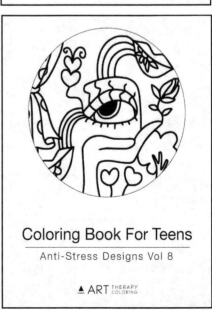

Coloring Book For Teens
Anti-Stress Designs Vol 8

ART THERAPY COLORING

Coloring Books For Adults

Coloring Books For Adults

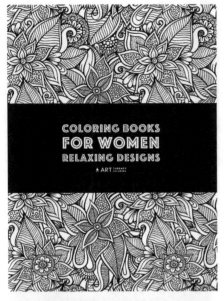

COLORING BOOKS
FOR WOMEN
RELAXING DESIGNS
ART THERAPY COLORING

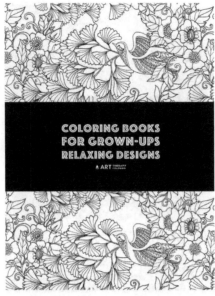

COLORING BOOKS
FOR GROWN-UPS
RELAXING DESIGNS
ART THERAPY COLORING

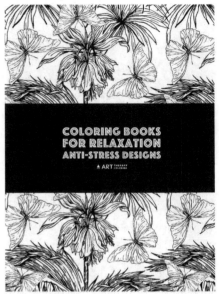

COLORING BOOKS
FOR RELAXATION
ANTI-STRESS DESIGNS
ART THERAPY COLORING

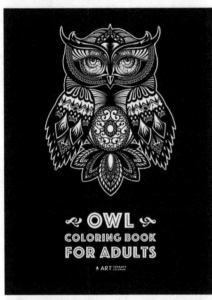

OWL
COLORING BOOK
FOR ADULTS
ART THERAPY COLORING

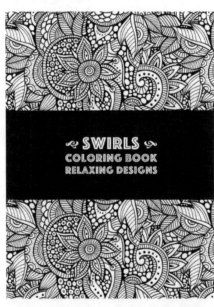

SWIRLS
COLORING BOOK
RELAXING DESIGNS

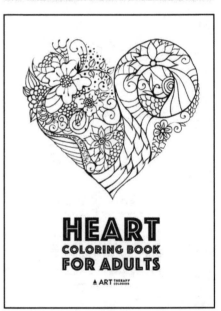

HEART
COLORING BOOK
FOR ADULTS
ART THERAPY COLORING

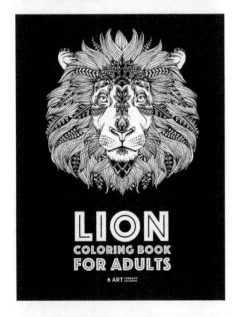

LION
COLORING BOOK
FOR ADULTS
ART THERAPY COLORING

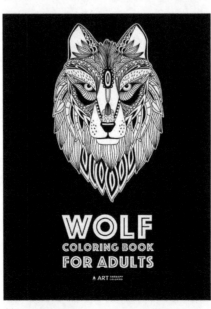

WOLF
COLORING BOOK
FOR ADULTS
ART THERAPY COLORING

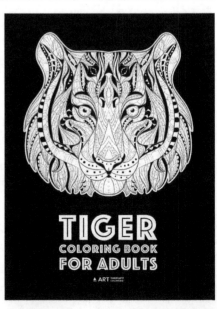

TIGER
COLORING BOOK
FOR ADULTS
ART THERAPY COLORING

Coloring Books For Men

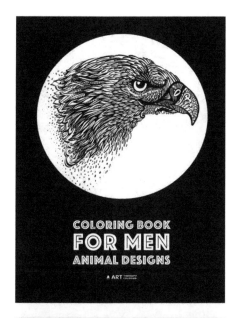

COLORING BOOK
FOR MEN
ANIMAL DESIGNS
ART THERAPY COLORING

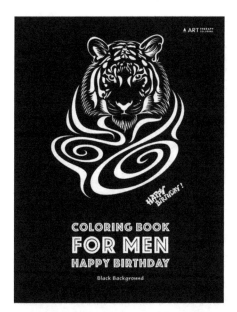

COLORING BOOK
FOR MEN
HAPPY BIRTHDAY
Black Background

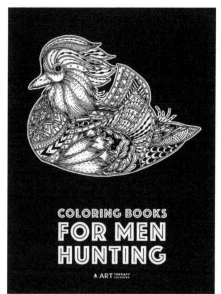

COLORING BOOKS
FOR MEN
HUNTING
ART THERAPY COLORING

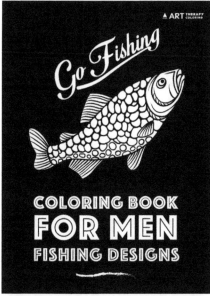

COLORING BOOK
FOR MEN
FISHING DESIGNS

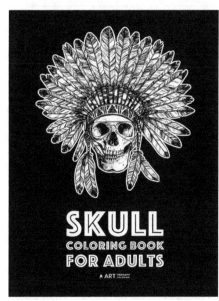

SKULL
COLORING BOOK
FOR ADULTS
ART THERAPY COLORING

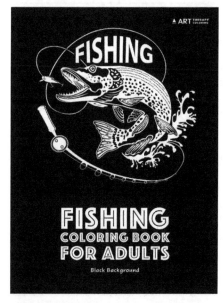

FISHING
COLORING BOOK
FOR ADULTS
Black Background

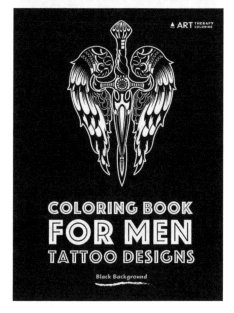

COLORING BOOK
FOR MEN
TATTOO DESIGNS
Black Background

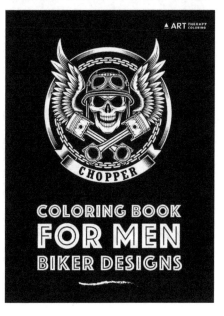

COLORING BOOK
FOR MEN
BIKER DESIGNS

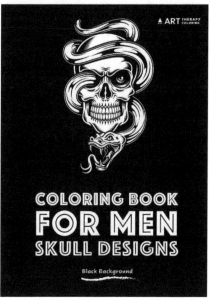

COLORING BOOK
FOR MEN
SKULL DESIGNS
Black Background

Coloring Books For Seniors

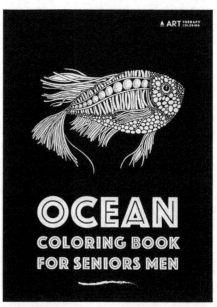

Coloring Books For Special Occasions

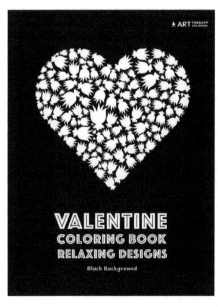

Coloring Books For Christmas

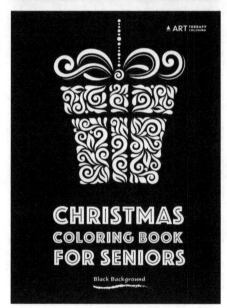

Coloring Books For Girls
Animal Designs

Published by:
Art Therapy Coloring
El Dorado Hills, California
www.arttherapycoloring.com

Shutterstock Images

ISBN: 978-1-64126-034-3

CPSIA information can be obtained
at www.ICGtesting.com
Printed in the USA
LVHW01s1846201217
560401LV00007B/787/P